Juan Diego

Mary's Humble Messenger

> 1474–1548
> Born near present-day
> Mexico City, Mexico
> Feast Day: December 9

Text by Barbara Yoffie
Illustrated by Katherine A. Borgatti

One Liguori Drive
Liguori MO 63057-9999

Dedication

To my family:
my parents Jim and Peg,
my husband Bill,
our son Sam and daughter-in-law Erin,
and our precious grandchildren
Ben, Lucas, and Andrew

To all the children I have had the privilege of
teaching throughout the years.

Imprimi Potest:
Harry Grile, CSsR, Provincial
Denver Province, The Redemptorists

Published by Liguori Publications
Liguori, Missouri 63057

To order, call 800-325-9521
www.liguori.org

Copyright © 2012 Liguori Publications

All rights reserved. No part of this publication may be reproduced, stored in a retrieval system, or transmitted in any form or by any means—electronic, mechanical, photocopy, recording, or any other—except for brief quotations in printed reviews, without the prior written permission of Liguori Publications.

ISBN 978-0-7648-2238-4

Liguori Publications, a nonprofit corporation, is an apostolate of The Redemptorists. To learn more about The Redemptorists, visit Redemptorists.com.

Printed in the United States of America
16 15 14 13 12 / 5 4 3 2 1
First Edition

Dear Parents and Teachers:

Saints and Me! is a series of children's books about saints. Six books make up the first set: *Saints of North America*. In this set, each book tells a thought-provoking story about a heavenly hero.

Saints of North America includes the heroic lives of six saints from the United States, Canada, and Mexico. Saints Kateri Tekakwitha and Elizabeth Ann Seton were both born in the United States. Saint Juan Diego was born in Mexico, and Saint André Bessette was from Canada. European missionaries also came to North America to spread the Catholic faith, making it their home while they worked with people in the New World. Saints Rose Philippine Duchesne and Damien de Veuster were missionary saints.

Through the centuries, saints have always been dear to Catholics, but *why*? In most instances, ordinary people were and are transformed by the life of Jesus and therefore model Christ's life for us. It is our Lord who makes ordinary people extraordinary. As your children come to know the saints, it is our hope that they will come to understand and identify that they, too, are *called to be saints*.

Which saint wanted to work with Native Americans? Who wanted to work with the sick people on the island of Molokai, Hawaii? To which saint did the Virgin Mary appear? Who loved Saint Joseph? Which saint started the first American religious community of women? Do you know which saint is the patron of nature? Find the answers in the *Saints of North America, Saints and Me!* set and help your child identify with the lives of the saints.

Introduce your children or students to the *Saints and Me!* series as they:

—**READ** about the lives of the saints and are inspired by their stories.

—**PRAY** to the saints for their intercession.

—**CELEBRATE** the saints and relate to their lives.

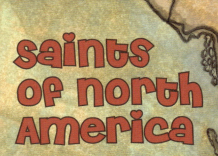

Saints of North America

- Kateri Tekakwitha
- Juan Diego
- Rose Philippine Duchesne
- Damien of Molokai
- Elizabeth Ann Seton
- André Bessette

Belgium

Juan Diego was born near present-day Mexico City, Mexico. He was a poor Aztec Indian. The Aztec Indians were treated unkindly by their rulers. But Juan found peace in the Catholic faith. Juan liked to pray and go to Mass.

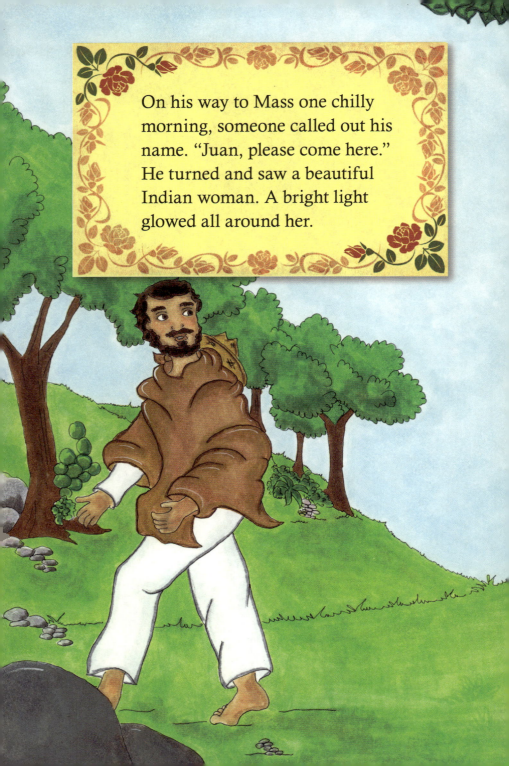

On his way to Mass one chilly morning, someone called out his name. "Juan, please come here." He turned and saw a beautiful Indian woman. A bright light glowed all around her.

"Hello, Juan. I am Mary, the Mother of God. I want a church built here for the people of Mexico. And I want you to tell the bishop to build it."

Juan rubbed his eyes and looked at the woman.
"It is the Virgin Mary!
I must do what she asks."
Off he ran to the city
to see the bishop.

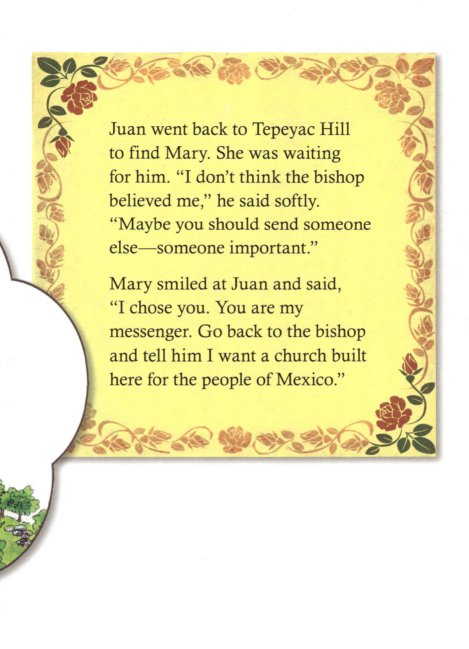

Juan went back to Tepeyac Hill to find Mary. She was waiting for him. "I don't think the bishop believed me," he said softly. "Maybe you should send someone else—someone important."

Mary smiled at Juan and said, "I chose you. You are my messenger. Go back to the bishop and tell him I want a church built here for the people of Mexico."

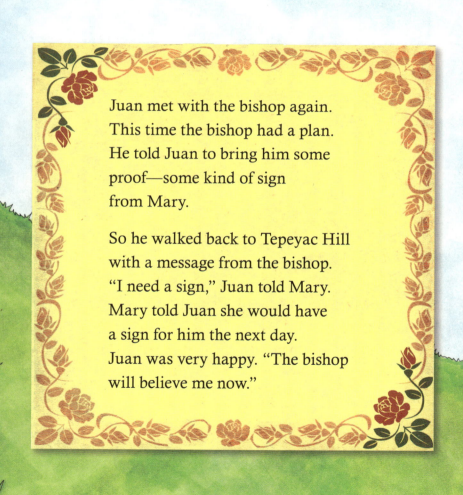

Juan met with the bishop again. This time the bishop had a plan. He told Juan to bring him some proof—some kind of sign from Mary.

So he walked back to Tepeyac Hill with a message from the bishop. "I need a sign," Juan told Mary. Mary told Juan she would have a sign for him the next day. Juan was very happy. "The bishop will believe me now."

The next day Juan hurried to see the Virgin Mary. Mary told Juan, "I have a sign for the bishop. Go to the top of the hill and you will see." Juan saw roses—dozens of beautiful roses. He put them in his cape and ran as fast as he could to the bishop's house.

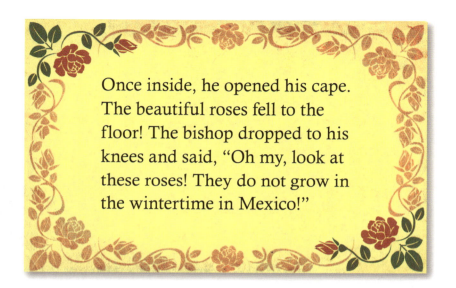

Once inside, he opened his cape. The beautiful roses fell to the floor! The bishop dropped to his knees and said, "Oh my, look at these roses! They do not grow in the wintertime in Mexico!"

Then the bishop pointed to Juan's cape. "It is a picture of the Virgin Mary. She looks like an Aztec princess. There is an angel, the moon, and many stars. This is a sign from heaven."

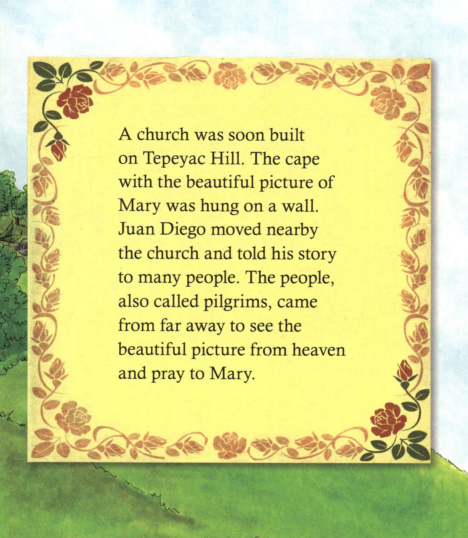

A church was soon built on Tepeyac Hill. The cape with the beautiful picture of Mary was hung on a wall. Juan Diego moved nearby the church and told his story to many people. The people, also called pilgrims, came from far away to see the beautiful picture from heaven and pray to Mary.

Today there is a very large church there. It is the Basilica of Our Lady of Guadalupe. Millions of pilgrims visit the church each year. It is a sign of Mary's love for the people of Mexico.

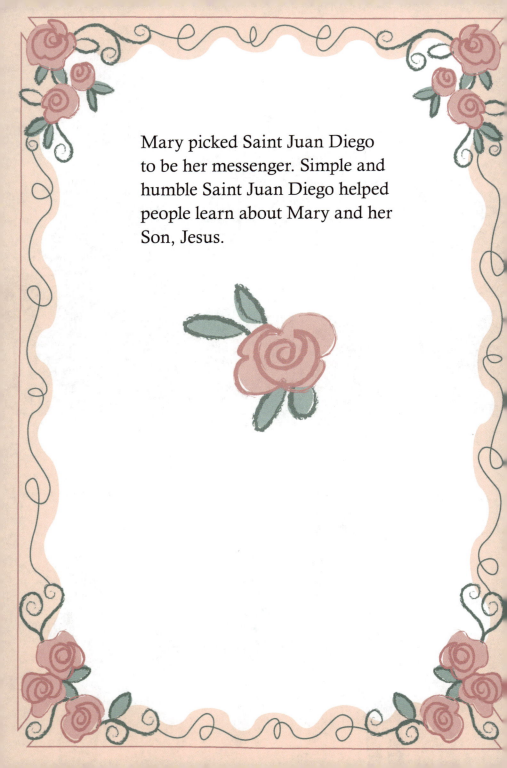

Mary picked Saint Juan Diego to be her messenger. Simple and humble Saint Juan Diego helped people learn about Mary and her Son, Jesus.

*Share your faith to show you care.
Spread God's message everywhere.*

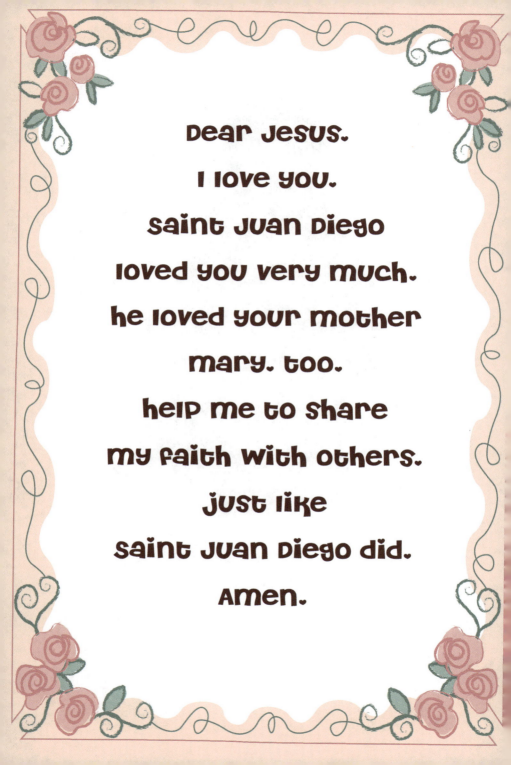

NEW WORDS (Glossary)

Aztec Indians: The Native American people who lived in Mexico

Basilica: A special and very large church

Bishop: A priest who is the leader of many churches in a certain area

Messenger: A person who takes a message to someone else

Our Lady of Guadalupe: Another name for Mary, the Mother of Jesus. When she appeared to Juan Diego in Mexico she was called Our Lady of Guadalupe.

Pilgrim: A person who travels to a holy place to pray

Sign: An object or event that has a message. For example, the Virgin Mary's picture on Juan Diego's cape was a special sign from God.

Liguori Publications
Saints and Me! Series
SAINTS OF NORTH AMERICA

Available now!
Kateri Tekakwitha
Model of Bravery

Available May 2013:

Rose Philippine Duchesne

Damien of Molokai

Elizabeth Ann Seton

André Bessette

Coming March 2013:

Saints of North America Activity Book

Reproducible activities
for all 6 saints in the series